Disney • PIXAR
TOY STORY 3

Toy-tastic Story

Read the story, then flip the book over to complete some awesome activities!

First published by Parragon in 2012
Parragon
Queen Street House
4 Queen Street
Bath BA1 1HE, UK
www.parragon.com

Edited by Samantha Crockford
Designed by Karl Tall
Production by Sarah Brown

ISBN 978-1-4454-4804-6
Printed in China

Disney · PIXAR

TOY STORY 3

Wild West Showdown!

Bath · New York · Singapore · Hong Kong · Cologne · Delhi
Melbourne · Amsterdam · Johannesburg · Auckland · Shenzhen

From the top of a high cliff, Sheriff Woody watched a train rumble across the desert.

Suddenly – **KA-BLAM!** The roof of one of the train cars exploded. The outlaw, One-Eyed Bart, climbed out, carrying bags of stolen money. Woody grabbed his lasso and leapt into action.

DISNEY · PIXAR

TOY STORY

Awesome Activities

Complete the activities, then flip the book over to read a toy-tastic story!

PaRragon

Bath · New York · Singapore · Hong Kong · Cologne · Delhi
Melbourne · Amsterdam · Johannesburg · Auckland · Shenzhen

Sheriff Woody

Woody the cowboy doll is Andy's favourite toy. Use this picture as a guide to colour Woody on the next page.

Shadow match

Can you match each toy to its shadow?

1

2

A

B

3

4

C

D

Answers on page 31

4

Eye spy!

Can you match each close-up to its owner?

1

2

3

A

B

C

Answers on page 31

Buzz Lightyear!

Buzz is a heroic space ranger action figure. Use this picture as a guide to colour Buzz on the opposite page.

Lasso laughs

Jessie has been trying to lasso Bullseye, but the ropes have got tangled up! Which one leads to Bullseye?

1 2 3

Answer on page 31

Sunnyside memory test

Have a close look at this picture. Count to ten, then turn over the page and see if you can pass the memory test!

Sunnyside memory test

Did you look closely at the picture on the previous page? There are five things missing from this picture. Can you tell what they are?

Answers on page 31

How many words?

Lotso smells like strawberries! How many words can you make from the letters in...

Strawberry?

Answers on page 31

Draw Buzz!

Look at this picture of Buzz, then use the grid on the opposite page to draw him yourself. You can also colour him in!

How many Hamms?

How many pictures of Hamm can you count?
Write your answer in the box below.

Answer:

Answer on page 31

Dinosaur search!

How many times can you find **REX** in the word grid? Look up, down, backwards, forwards and diagonally. Write your answer in the box below.

Answers on page 31

```
R O X E R E R G
E I E X E R E O
X E R Z X R X D
G I Z E Y I T S
X I R J X E R A
E E A E G E E R
R M R T X R X E
S H B R E X F X
```

Answer:

Playtime!

Colour this picture of Jessie, Buzz and Woody enjoying playtime at Andy's house.

The bad guys

The Aliens and Hamm love playing the baddies at playtime! Is Rex about to catch them?

17

Shadow match

Match each of these Sunnyside Daycare residents to its shadow.

1

2

A

B

3

4

C

D

Answers on page 31

Hide and seek

Mr Potato Head has challenged Slinky Dog to a game of hide and seek. Help Mr Potato Head through the maze so he can find his friend.

Answers on page 31

19

Sunnyside looks strange!

Look closely at this picture of the Sunnyside Daycare. There are eight objects that don't belong there! Can you find them and circle them?

Answers on page 31

Sunnyside search!

These objects DO belong at Sunnyside.
Can you find and circle them
in the picture?

1 Mobile

2 Books

3 Light switches

4 Ball

5 Sparks

6 Twitch

7 Butterfly

8 Marbles

Answers on page 31

21

Go dotty!

Howdy, partner! Complete the picture by connecting the dots. Then colour it in.

Start Here!

Answers on page 31

Playtime puzzle

Answer the questions to complete the crossword below.

2 ↓

3 →

1 → 4 X G

1. Slinky Dog's body is made of a...
2. Buzz is a toy space...
3. Lots-o'-Huggin' Bear smells of...

Answers on page 31

Guess the toys

Look at the close-ups and see if you can guess which toys they belong to!

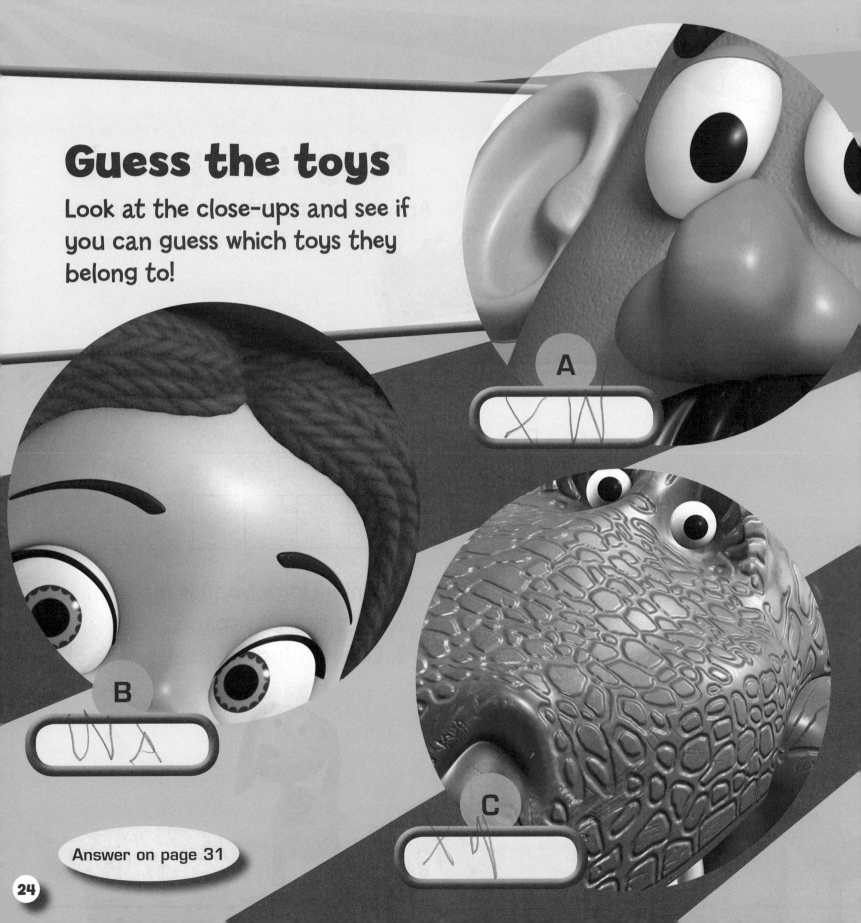

A

B

C

Answer on page 31

24

Spot the difference

Look closely at these two pictures. Can you spot six things that have changed in the second picture?

Answers on page 31

To the rescue!

Buzz has got lost in the middle of a maze! Find the correct path to Buzz so that Jessie can rescue him.

Answers on page 31

Seeing double

Take a look at these pictures of Bullseye. Can you tell which two are the same?

1

2

3

4

5

6

Answers on page 31

A new home

Andy knows it's time to pass on his favourite toys. Bonnie already loves them! Colour this picture.

Goodbye Andy!

Buzz and Woody are saying goodbye to Andy. Colour this picture of the best friends.

Look who's talking

Can you match each toy
to its catchphrase?

1

3

2

4

"Howdy partner!"
A

"To infinity and beyond!"
B

"Roar!"
C

"OoOOOoh!"
D

Answers on page 31

Answers

Page 4

1-C
2-D
3-B
4-A

Page 5

1-C
2-A
3-B

Page 8

3

Page 10

Page 11

Strawberry?

A few examples are:
raw, sat, bat, rat, war, yet, star, rare, tray, straw, berry.

If you got more than 10, you're a super speller. If not, keep going!

Page 14

9

Page 15

17 times

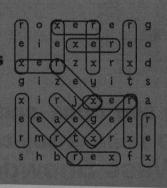

Page 18

1-C

2-D

3-B

4-A

Page 19

Page 20

Andy's picture, bathtub, flying fish, campfire, knight in armour, a chandelier, spaghetti and a dragon.

Page 21

Page 23

S T R A W B E R R I E S

S P R I N G (STRANGER)

Page 24

A-Mr Potato Head

B-Jessie

C-Rex

Page 25

Page 26

Page 27

3 and 4

Page 30

1-B
2-A
3-C
4-D

Now close the book and flip it over to read a toy-tastic story – Wild West Showdown!

Now close the book and **flip it over** to complete some **awesome activities!**

The End

Soon, the villains were all tied up ready to go to jail. "Good job, deputies!" Woody shouted. The Sheriff and his friends had saved the day again!

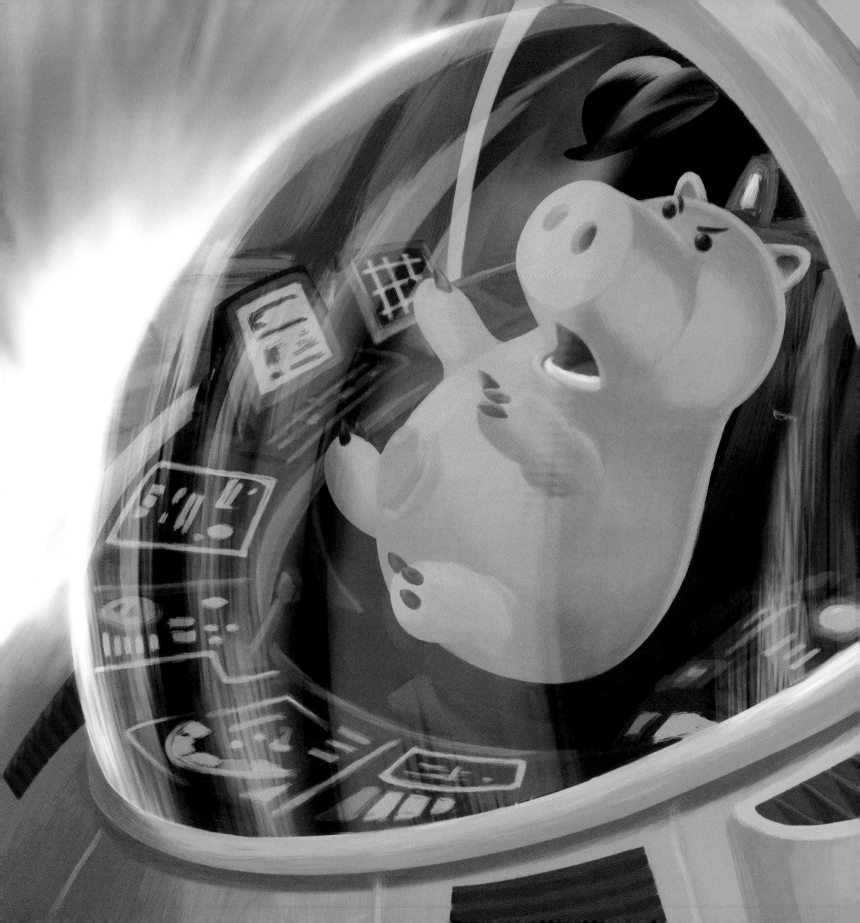

"Buzz!" shouted Woody above the screeching monkeys. "Shoot your laser at my badge!"

"Woody, no!" cried Buzz. "It will kill you!"

"Just do it!" yelled Woody.

Buzz aimed his laser beam at Woody's badge and fired. The beam bounced off the badge and hit Dr Porkchop's spaceship. **BOOM!**

"That's *Mister* Evil Dr Porkchop to you!" yelled the villain from behind the control panel.

With a wicked laugh, Dr Porkchop pressed a button and dropped an army of vicious monkeys onto Woody, Jessie and Buzz.

27

But before the dinosaur could attack, a giant shadow appeared overhead. A pig-shaped spaceship beamed One-Eyed Bart, Betty and their sidekicks to safety.

"Evil Dr Porkchop!" cried Woody.

"Well, I brought my dinosaur, who *eats* force-field dogs!" replied Woody.

"Yodel-lay-hee-hoooooo!" yodelled Jessie.

A gigantic dinosaur burst out of the ground with a ferocious **ROAR!**

Suddenly, a giant dog with a metal coil for a body surrounded the outlaws.

"You can't touch me, Sheriff!" shouted One-Eyed Bart. "I brought my attack dog, who has a built-in force field!"

Buzz swooped down and used his laser to slice One-Eyed Bart's getaway car in half. Bart, Betty and their Alien sidekicks tumbled out onto the ground.

Suddenly, Buzz Lightyear, the space ranger, appeared! He flew beneath the train and lifted it out of the canyon.

"Glad you could catch the train, Buzz!" shouted Woody.

Jessie and Bullseye cheered with delight as Buzz carried the train to safety.

"Now let's catch some criminals!" said Buzz.

The train came to a screeching halt – but not soon enough. It plummeted into the canyon with Woody and the orphans still on board.

"No!" Jessie cried.

"Hurry!" yelled Jessie.

The train was speeding towards the canyon! Woody quickly found the brake and pulled on it as hard as he could.

"Ride like the wind, Bullseye!" Woody shouted. He had to save the orphans before going after One-Eyed Bart.

When the brave horse reached the front of the train, Woody leapt onto the engine.

"Give it up, Bart!" Woody called. "You've reached the end of the line."

But One-Eyed Bart wouldn't be stopped that easily. He pulled out a detonator and pressed the button.

KABOOM! A bridge that spanned a giant canyon was blown to pieces. Bart and Betty jumped into their getaway car.

"It's me or the kiddies!" yelled One-Eyed Bart. "Take your pick!"

As the outlaws sped away, Jessie looked up and saw that the train was filled with orphans – and it was heading straight towards the blown-up bridge!

"Ai-ai-ai-ai-ai-yah!" came a cry from behind Woody. It was One-Eyed Betty – One-Eyed Bart's karate-chopping wife! Betty charged, knocking Woody right off the train.
"Ahh!" cried Woody.
Suddenly, Jessie the cowgirl came speeding up on her trusty steed, Bullseye. They caught Woody just in time!

"You've got a date with justice, One-Eyed Bart!" cried Sheriff Woody.

The surprised bandit stopped in his tracks and dropped the bags of money at Woody's feet.